W9-CJZ-194

SKY TERRORS

by Natalie Lunis

Consultant: Luis M. Chiappe, Ph.D.
Director of the Dinosaur Institute
Natural History Museum of Los Angeles County

PUBLISHING

NEW YORK, NEW YORK

Credits

Title Page, © Luis Rey; TOC-L, © Anness Publishing/The Natural History Museum, London; TOC-R, © Gareth Monger; 4-5, © John Bindon; 6, © Anness Publishing/The Natural History Museum, London; 7, © Luis Rey; 8, © John Bindon; 9, © Luis Rey; 10, © Luis Rey; 11, © John Bindon; 12, © Gareth Monger; 13, © Anness Publishing/The Natural History Museum, London; 14, © Michael W. Skrepnick; 15, © Luis Rey; 16, © 2007 Black Hills Institute of Geological Research, Photographer: Timothy Larson; 17, © John Sibbick; 18, © Phil Wilson; 19, © Phil Wilson; 20, © The Art Archive/Bibliothèque de l'Assemblée Nationale Paris/Mireille Vautier; 21, © Luis Rey; 23TL, © Michael W. Skrepnick; 23TR, © Luis Rey; 23BL, © Vladimir Sazonov/Shutterstock; 23BR, © Luis Rey.

Publisher: Kenn Goin
Editorial Director: Adam Siegel
Creative Director: Spencer Brinker
Design: Dawn Beard Creative
Cover Illustration: Luis Rey
Photo Researcher: Omni-Photo Communications, Inc.

Library of Congress Cataloging-in-Publication Data

Lunis, Natalie.
  Sky terrors / by Natalie Lunis.
     p. cm. — (Dino times trivia)
  Includes bibliographical references and index.
  ISBN-13: 978-1-59716-714-7 (lib. bdg.)
  ISBN-10: 1-59716-714-2 (lib. bdg.)
  1. Pterosauria—Juvenile literature. I. Title.

QE862.P7L86 2009
567.918—dc22
                          2008014265

For more information, write to Bearport Publishing Company, Inc., 101 Fifth Avenue, Suite 6R, New York, New York 10003. Printed in the United States of America.

10 9 8 7 6 5 4 3 2 1

Contents

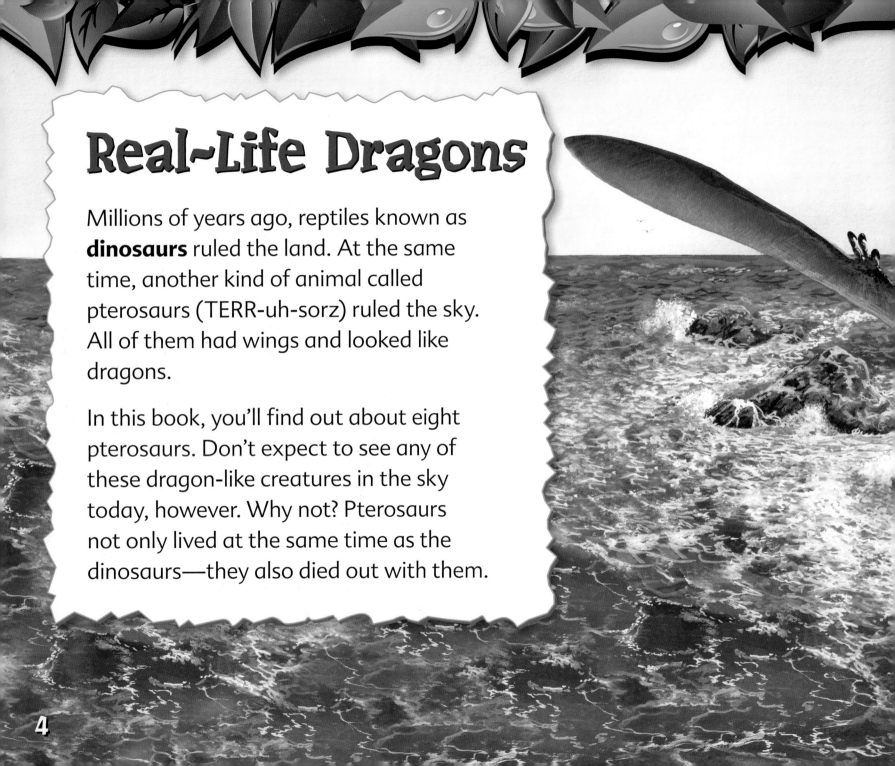

Real~Life Dragons

Millions of years ago, reptiles known as **dinosaurs** ruled the land. At the same time, another kind of animal called pterosaurs (TERR-uh-sorz) ruled the sky. All of them had wings and looked like dragons.

In this book, you'll find out about eight pterosaurs. Don't expect to see any of these dragon-like creatures in the sky today, however. Why not? Pterosaurs not only lived at the same time as the dinosaurs—they also died out with them.

There were many kinds of pterosaurs. Some were only the size of a sparrow. Others were as large as a small plane.

Dsungaripterus

How do you say it?

jung-uh-RIP-ter-uhss

What does it mean?

Junggar wing

(named after the Junggar Basin, the place in China where its bones were first found)

How big was it?

Dsungaripterus could fly like a bird. It could flap its wings as well as glide through the air.

Was *Dsungaripterus* a kind of bird that lived long ago?

No. *Dsungaripterus* and all other pterosaurs were closely related to birds and were like them in many ways. However, all pterosaurs were flying reptiles—not birds.

The word *pterosaur* means "flying reptile."

Eudimorphodon

How do you say it?
yoo-dye-MOR-fuh-don

What does it mean?
true two-tooth form

How big was it?

meters		feet
3 —		— 10
		— 8
2 —		— 6
		— 4
1 —		— 2
0 —		— 0

Eudimorphodon had wings. However, its wings were different from a bird's. They didn't have any feathers. The wings were covered just with skin.

In what other important way was *Eudimorphodon* different from any bird living today?

Eudimorphodon had teeth in its jaws. No bird living today has teeth.

8

Pterodactylus

How do you say it?
terr-uh-DAK-tuh-luhss

What does it mean?
wing finger

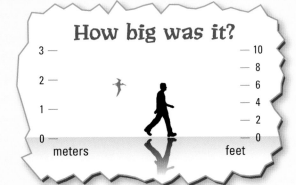

Pterodactylus has a name that means "wing finger."

Why did scientists give it this name?

On each wing, *Pterodactylus* had a very long fourth finger. The bones of this finger were inside the wing and helped hold the wing's shape.

wing fingers

10

Rhamphorhynchus

How do you say it?
ram-for-INK-uhss

What does it mean?
beak jaw

Rhamphorhynchus had a long tail that was shaped like a paddle at the end. So did many other pterosaurs.

Did this tail have any special use?

Yes. *Rhamphorhynchus* could tilt its tail in different ways when flying. Moving its tail in this way helped it steer.

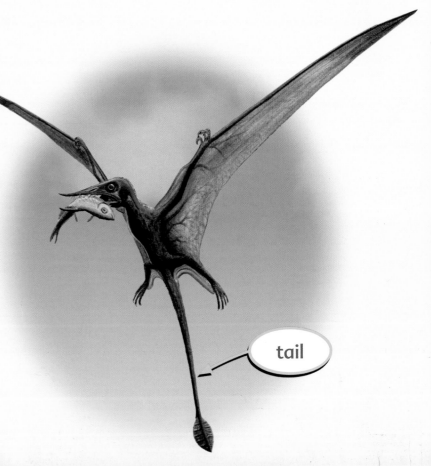

tail

12

tail

Not all pterosaurs had long tails. In fact, scientists divide flying reptiles into two groups—those with long tails and those with short tails.

Pteranodon

How do you say it?
tuh-RAN-uh-don

What does it mean?
toothless flyer

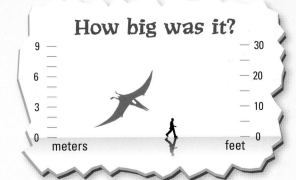

How big was it?

Pteranodon was one of the largest pterosaurs. It did not have a long tail, but it did have a large **crest** on top of its head.

How did the crest help *Pteranodon*?

The crest helped *Pteranodon* steer as it flew—just like a long tail helped *Rhamphorhynchus* steer.

crest

Dorygnathus

How do you say it?
dor-ig-NAY-thuhss

What does it mean?
spear jaw

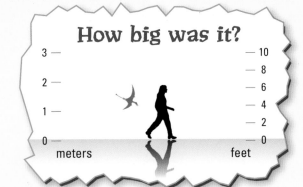

How big was it?

3 —		— 10
		— 8
2 —		— 6
		— 4
1 —		— 2
0 —		— 0
meters		feet

Dorygnathus lived near the ocean. It had a set of long, sharp, curved teeth that stuck out of its mouth.

How did these teeth help *Dorygnathus* get its food?

The long, sharp, curved teeth of *Dorygnathus* helped it grab and hold the slippery fish that it caught as it swooped down on the water.

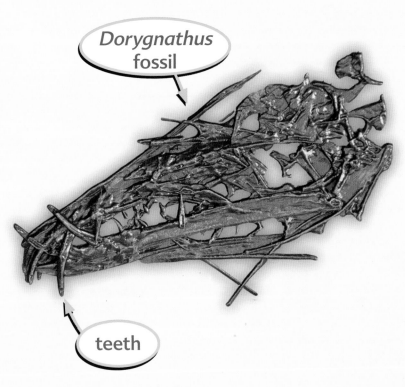

Dorygnathus fossil

teeth

16

Scientists think that most pterosaurs lived near the ocean. Why? Most of the pterosaur **fossils** they have found were buried in places that were once under or near ocean waters.

Pterodaustro

How do you say it?
terr-uh-DAW-stroh

What does it mean?
wing of the south

How big was it?

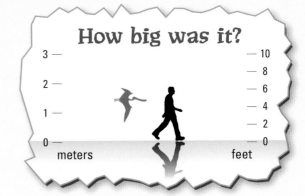

3 — / — 10
— 8
2 — / — 6
— 4
1 — / — 2
0 — / — 0
meters   feet

teeth

Pterodaustro had a lower jaw with hundreds of long, thin teeth that were all very close together. They looked like the teeth of a comb.

How did *Pterodaustro*'s strange-looking teeth help it eat?

Pterodaustro ate tiny creatures that lived in lakes. To get them, it scooped up a mouthful of water. Then it squeezed the water out through its teeth and swallowed the tiny creatures that were left behind.

18

Today some whales and sharks eat in a way that is similar to the way Pterodaustro ate.

19

Quetzalcoatlus

How do you say it?
kwet-zal-koh-AHT-luhss

What does it mean?
feathered snake

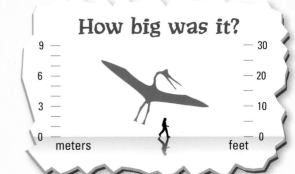

How big was it?

Quetzalcoatlus was the biggest flying animal that ever lived. It had a **wingspan** of 40 feet (12 m)—about the same as a small plane.

How could such a big animal stay up in the air?

Quetzalcoatlus had light, hollow bones. All flying animals, including pterosaurs, birds, and bats, need lightweight bones to keep their bodies from being too heavy for flight.

Quetzalcoatl

Quetzalcoatlus was named after Quetzalcoatl, a god of the Aztec people of ancient Mexico. Quetzalcoatl looked like a feathered snake.

20

wingspan

Where Did They Live?

This map shows some of the places where the fossils of pterosaurs have been found.

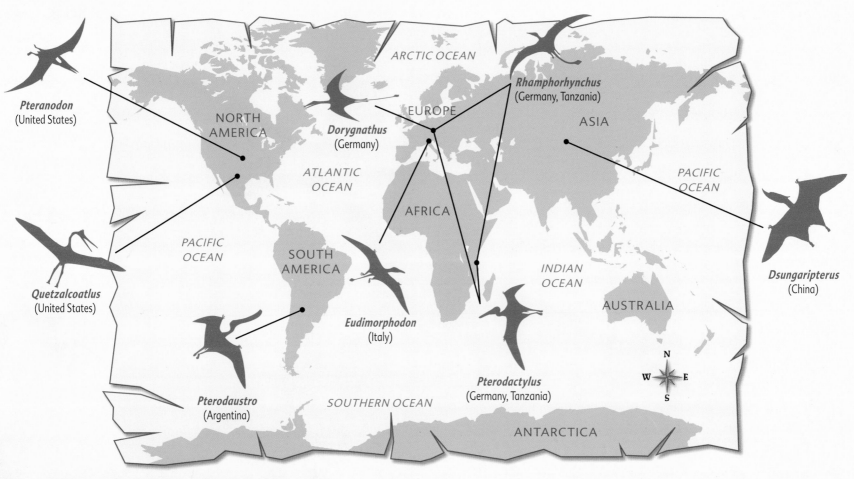

Pteranodon
(United States)

ARCTIC OCEAN

EUROPE

Rhamphorhynchus
(Germany, Tanzania)

Dorygnathus
(Germany)

ASIA

NORTH AMERICA

ATLANTIC OCEAN

PACIFIC OCEAN

Quetzalcoatlus
(United States)

PACIFIC OCEAN

SOUTH AMERICA

AFRICA

Dsungaripterus
(China)

Eudimorphodon
(Italy)

INDIAN OCEAN

AUSTRALIA

N W E S

Pterodaustro
(Argentina)

SOUTHERN OCEAN

Pterodactylus
(Germany, Tanzania)

ANTARCTICA

When Did They Live?

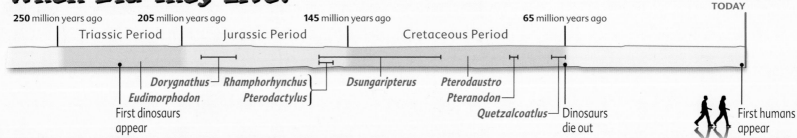

250 million years ago	205 million years ago	145 million years ago	65 million years ago	TODAY
Triassic Period	Jurassic Period	Cretaceous Period		

Dorygnathus   **Rhamphorhynchus**   **Dsungaripterus**   **Pterodaustro**

Eudimorphodon   **Pterodactylus**   **Pteranodon**

First dinosaurs appear

Quetzalcoatlus — Dinosaurs die out

First humans appear

Glossary

crest (KREST) bone, feathers, or skin on top of an animal's head

dinosaurs (DYE-nuh-sorz) reptiles that lived on land more than 65 million years ago, and then died out

fossils (FOSS-uhlz) what is left of plants or animals that lived long ago

wingspan (WING-*span*) the distance between the tips of wings

Index

Read More

Brown, Charlotte Lewis. *Beyond the Dinosaurs: Monsters of the Air and Sea.* New York: HarperCollins (2007).

Hughes, Monica. *Flying Giants.* New York: Bearport Publishing (2008).

Lessem, Don. *Flying Giants of Dinosaur Time.* Minneapolis, MN: Lerner Publishing (2005).

Learn More Online

To learn more about pterosaurs, visit
www.bearportpublishing.com/DinoTimesTrivia

About the Author

Natalie Lunis has written more than 30 science and nature books for children. She lives in the New York City area.